by Susan Sinnott

Content Adviser: Professor Sherry L. Field,
Department of Social Science Education, College of Education,
The University of Georgia

Reading Adviser: Dr. Linda D. Labbo,
Department of Reading Education, College of Education,
The University of Georgia

Compass Point Books ✦ Minneapolis, Minnesota

Compass Point Books
1710 Roe Crest Drive
North Mankato, MN 56003

Visit Compass Point Books on the Internet at *www.capstonepub.com*

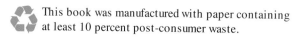 This book was manufactured with paper containing
at least 10 percent post-consumer waste.

Photographs ©: Photo Network/Phyllis Picardi, cover; International Stock/Orion, 4; International Stock/R.M.
Arakaki, 6; Toyohiro Yamada/FPG International, 7; Unicorn Stock Photos/Jeff Greenberg, 8; Travelpix/FPG
International, 9; Toyohiro Yamada/FPG International, 10; Visuals Unlimited/Ken Lucas, 11; Unicorn Stock
Photos/Jean Higgins, 12; Photo Network/Bachmann, 13; North Wind Picture Archives, 14; Unicorn Stock
Photos/Deborah L. Martin, 16; Bettmann/Corbis, 17, 18, 19; Archive Photos, 20, 21, 22; Unicorn Stock
Photos/Tommy Dodson, 23 top; T. Zimmerman/FPG International, 23 bottom; David Wade/FPG International,
24; Reuters/Erico Sugita/Archive Photos, 25; Ace or Adrian Bradshow/Archive Photos, 26; Unicorn Stock
Photos/Paul A. Hein, 27; Reuters/Erico Sugita/Archive Photos, 28; Trip/Trip, 29; Jean Kugler/FPG
International 30; Robbie Jack/Corbis, 31; Unicorn Stock Photos/Ron P. Jaffe, 32; Michael S. Yamashita/Corbis,
33; VCG/FPG International, 34; Jeff Greenberg/Archive Photos, 35; Reuters/Mashaharu Hatano/Archive
Photos, 36 top; Photo Network/Ehlers, 36 bottom; Unicorn Stock Photos/Paul A. Hein, 37; International
Stock/Ronn Maratea, 38; Index Stock Imagery, 39; David Bartruff/FPG International, 40; David Wade/FPG
International, 41; Photo Network/Chad Ehlers, 42; International Stock/Chad Ehlers, 43; Norman Owen
Tomalin/Bruce Coleman, Inc., 45.

Editors: E. Russell Primm and Emily J. Dolbear
Photo Researcher: Svetlana Zhurkina
Photo Selector: Dawn Friedman
Design: Bradfordesign, Inc.
Cartography: XNR Productions, Inc.

Library of Congress Cataloging-in-Publication Data
Gray, Shirley W.
    Japan / by Susan Sinnott.
        p. cm. — (First reports)
    Includes bibliographical references and index.
    Summary: An introduction to the geography, history, culture, and people of Japan.
    ISBN 978-0-7565-0030-6 (library binding)
    ISBN 978-0-7565-1215-6 (paperback)
        1. Japan—Juvenile literature. [1. Japan.] I. Title. II. Series.
    DS806 .S56 2000
    952—dc21   00-008526

Printed in the United States of America in North Mankato, Minnesota.
082012   006881R

Table of Contents

"Konnichi wa!"

"Konnichi wa! Good day! Welcome to Japan!"

You might hear this greeting if you visit Japan.
The islands of Japan lie east of Russia, North Korea,

▲ *A Japanese family wearing traditional kimonos*

▲ Map of Japan

South Korea, and China in the North Pacific Ocean. It
is part of East Asia. The country is made up of four
main islands and almost 4,000 small islands.

▲ Mount Fuji and Fujiyoshida City

Some of Japan's islands have very high mountains.
Japan's highest peak is Mount Fuji, at 12,388 feet
(3,776 meters). Between the mountain areas are

▲ *Rice fields, or paddies*

broad, flat lands called **plains**. Today, most of Japan's people live on these plains.

▲ *Tokyo as seen from the air*

Tokyo is Japan's capital city. Tokyo, Osaka, and Yokohama are the largest cities.

▲ *Osaka has a mixture of old and new buildings.*

▲ *A passenger boat near the shore of Yoron*

To get away from the crowded cities, the Japanese go to the mountains or the seashore. Japan is a modern country, but its people take time to admire their country's natural gifts and follow its old traditions. The national bird is the beautiful red-crowned crane. The red-faced monkeys called Japanese macaques are also a special sight.

A red-crowned crane ▶

Emperors and Samurai

▲ Nara's Todaiji Temple is the largest wooden building in the world.

Japan is an old country with an interesting history. Long ago, Japan was not one country. It was made up of many small states at war with one another. By A.D. 700, one prince became powerful enough be the country's first ruler, or **emperor**. He made Nara the first capital city.

In A.D. 794, the capital was moved

▲ *Kinkakuji Temple in Kyoto*

to nearby Kyoto. Another emperor built glittering palaces and temples, but he wasn't a good leader. Local warlords and the emperor's army, called the **samurai,** often stepped in to manage things. The

▲ Samurai warriors

samurai generals were devoted to religion and protecting their honor. They were loyal to the death. Over time, they became powerful and often mistreated the people.

The samurai and the warlords fought off enemies from other parts of Asia. The most feared leader was Kublai Khan from Mongolia. He had named himself emperor of China. In 1281, Kublai Khan's ships reached the coast of Japan. As they came ashore, a great wind suddenly smashed the ships to bits. The Japanese called this wind *Kamikaze*. They still call for it when their country is in danger.

Cutting Off Contact

The 1400s marked the end of Kyoto as Japan's capital city. As the samurai generals, the warlords, and the emperor fought for power, fire almost destroyed the city.

▲ *The grounds of the Imperial Palace in Tokyo*

In 1603, a new emperor finally ended the fighting. He moved the capital to the old city of Edo. Today, Edo is called Tokyo. Even after moving his palace to Tokyo, the emperor didn't feel safe. He believed that other nations wanted to take over Japan. He cut off all contact with other countries for 200 years.

In 1853, however, Commodore Matthew C. Perry of the U.S. Navy was sent to visit Japan. His ships sailed right into Edo Bay. The Japanese had never seen big, black, steam-powered ships before. They feared the worst, but Commander Perry's visit was friendly. The

▲ Commodore Matthew C. Perry

▲ *Commodore Perry's ships sailing into Tokyo*

Japanese ruler finally agreed to join the modern world. Soon Japan was trading goods with other countries.

▲ Japanese soldiers marched into Nanking, China, in 1937

The Japanese tried to become modern quickly. By the early 1900s, the country had strong military forces. In the 1930s, Japan took over parts of China. In 1939, Japan became friends with Germany.

▲ *Ships on fire after the Japanese attack on Pearl Harbor*

In 1939, World War II began in Europe. The United States warned Japan not to cause trouble for its neighbors. However, on December 7, 1941, Japan attacked the U.S. naval base at Pearl Harbor, Hawaii. The United States then declared war on Japan.

▲ *Above Hiroshima after the first atomic bomb was dropped*

In 1945, the United States dropped two atomic bombs—one on the Japanese city of Hiroshima, one on Nagasaki. Some 100,000 people were killed. The Japanese soon gave up.

▲ *Nagasaki after the bombing*

Japan rose up from the ruins of war, however. Once again, it is a world leader in **industry**. Japanese cars and electronic products are sold around the world. After the United States, Japan's industry and trade are the biggest in the world.

Peace Memorial Park
in Hiroshima ▶

▲ *A Japanese motorcycle plant*

Religion in Japan

▲ *Shinto priests enter the Meiji Shrine in Tokyo.*

The two major religions in Japan today are Shinto and Buddhism. Many people follow both religions. Thousands of temples and **shrines** were built in Japan. Many people visit them today.

Shinto is a set of beliefs. People who follow Shinto worship many gods called *kami*. They believe that kami link all things together—from humans to rocks to the sea. People make huge buildings, statues, or small displays in their homes called **shrines**, to honor kami.

Buddhism began in India. It came to Japan from China. Many Japanese believe in a kind of Buddhism called *Zen*, which means "**meditation**." Meditation is a way of focusing

▲ *A man meditates in his office building's Zen meditation room.*

your thoughts, usually while you are sitting or lying in a quiet place.

Several forms of art came from Zen Buddhism. One is the Way of Tea, a ceremony of making and serving tea. Samurai used to build special teahouses in their gardens where they could meditate and follow

▲ Japanese women performing the tea ceremony

the Way of Tea. Another art is flower arranging, called *ikebana*. The combination of flowers, leaves, branches, and vase show harmony among all things.

An example of ikebana ▶

Japanese Festivals

▲ *Thousands wait to make their New Year's prayers.*

The Japanese love festivals. *Shogatsu* (New Year) is celebrated on January 1 and lasts several days. March 3 brings *Hinamatsuri*, the doll festival. People display their old and sometimes valuable doll collections. Girls visit one another's houses, eat sweets, and admire the dolls. On May 5, a festival called

▲ *Two girls admire a doll collection during* Hinamatsuri.

Tango-no-Sekku takes place. Boys raise carp-shaped banners on poles near their houses. Inside, they display small models of samurai warriors.

Each February, people try to guess when the cherry trees will bloom. *Sakura zensen* (cherry blossom time) starts in late March and usually lasts until

▲ *Cherry trees bloom in a Kyoto park.*

mid-May. This is the favorite time of year for many Japanese. Everyone flocks to the country to picnic under the blossoming cherry trees.

Noh, Kabuki, and Bunraku

Theater has been part of Japanese culture since the time of the samurai. *Noh* theater mixes Shinto and Buddhist teachings. The actor performs on a bare stage wearing a mask that shows if he is happy or angry. He or she walks and dances slowly and never speaks. Singers sitting on

▲ *A Noh actor*

▲ *A Kabuki actor*

one side of the stage chant the story. Four musicians play traditional Japanese instruments.

While the emperor and nobles watched Noh plays, the common people flocked to see *Kabuki*. Kabuki theater also mixes drama and dance, but it is much livelier and very colorful. The stories are tales from Japanese history and legend. Kabuki actors are always men and often play women. The audience often shouts back at the actors on stage.

▲ Bunraku *puppet masters during a performance*

Bunraku is a puppet theater. Two or three puppet masters—all dressed in black—control life-size puppets. As the puppets move around on stage, a singer chants a familiar story.

City Life

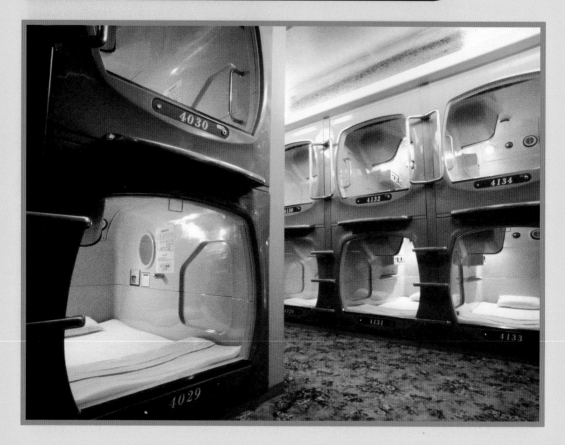

▲ *This hotel in Tokyo makes the most of limited space.*

Life in Japan's cities is crowded. Tokyo has some of the busiest streets in the world. It also has acres of beautiful, peaceful gardens. The Imperial Palace is only a few blocks away from Tokyo's business section.

▲ *Shoppers in Tokyo*

The palace, surrounded by water, was built on the grounds of a ruined castle.

On city streets in Japan, young people wear the most up-to-date fashions. For special occasions, however, they may still dress in a *kimono*, a one-piece, wraparound robe. Young people have to work hard in

Employees of the Tokyo Stock Exchange wear traditional kimonos for the opening day of trading.

▼ Japanese school girls

school. They go to class on Saturdays and wear uniforms! They enjoy their freedom and free time.

The Japanese Home

▲ *A Japanese home with futon beds*

Because so many people live in Japan's cities, the houses and apartments are very small. The Japanese furnish their homes so that the space seems bigger.

Many people have no tables or chairs in their houses. People sit on straw mats. Because the Japanese sit on the floor, no one is allowed to wear shoes inside the house. Instead of large beds, the Japanese often sleep on mattresses called futons. Futons are used on the floor and stored in closets at other times.

In most Japanese living rooms, there is a special shelf or corner for a painting, flower arrangement, or display of fine handwriting called calligraphy. These shelves are changed according to the season or festival.

▲ *A woman doing calligraphy*

Food in Japan

Traditionally, the Japanese like their food to look beautiful and taste good. They slice, shape, and display their vegetables to look like objects in a painting. Of course, people in a hurry often eat a meal from a noodle stand or fast-food restaurant.

▲ Sashimi, *a raw fish dish*

The Japanese eat lots of seafood, which is often served raw. Their raw fish dishes called *sushi* and *sashimi* have become popular around the world. Rice is served with most meals. Japanese people sit on the floor and eat with chopsticks at low tables.

Tea is served at every meal. Visitors are always offered tea. In fact, the Japanese word for "living room" is similar to the word for "tea room." When they are celebrating, the Japanese also drink a rice wine called *sake*.

▲ *People sit on the floor at a Japanese restaurant.*

Sports and Travel

▲ *Baseball fans at the stadium in Yokohama*

Baseball is a national sport in Japan. People also enjoy watching and playing golf and tennis. But sumo wrestling is a truly Japanese sport. The wrestlers often weigh more than 300 pounds (136 kilograms). Their

▲ *Sumo wrestlers face the crowd before a match.*

trainer is a sumo master. Wrestlers face off in a ring and try to make the other wrestler fall. Nearly half a million Japanese men belong to sumo clubs, but only a few have any chance to become *yokozuna* (grand champion).

The Japanese love to travel in their country and around the world. They relax in hot springs on their own island of Kyushu and visit Australia, Europe, the United States, and Hong Kong. In turn, millions of tourists visit Japan each year.

If you visit, you will learn more about this East Asian country. As you leave, you will probably say, "*Domo arigato!* Thank you. I enjoyed my visit to Japan."

▲ *Beppu Hot Spring on Kyushu*

Glossary

emperor—male ruler

industry—a business that makes products

meditation— a way of focusing your thoughts, usually while you are sitting or lying in a quiet place

plains—broad, flat land

samurai—Japanese warriors

shrines—small displays built to honor a god

Did You Know?

- Japan often suffers violent earthquakes. In 1995, an earthquake in Kobe killed more than 6,000 people.

- During rush hours in Tokyo, trains are so crowded that the subways hire "pushers"—people who push as many people as they can onto the trains.

- Japan's long coastline stretches 18,490 miles (29,750 kilometers).

At a Glance

Official name: *Nippon* or *Nihon* (Land of the Rising Sun)

Capital: Tokyo

Official language(s): Japanese

National song: *"Kimigayo"* ("Our Emperor's Reign")

Area: 145,884 square miles (377,840 square kilometers)

Highest point: Mount Fuji, 12,388 feet (3,776 meters) above sea level

Lowest point: sea level

Population: 127,417,244 (2005 estimate)

Head of government: Prime minister

Money: Yen

Important Dates

794 Kyoto becomes capital city.

1281 Kublai Khan's ships reach the coast of Japan.

1603 Emperor moves the capital city to Edo, now Tokyo, and cuts off contact with outside the world.

1853 Commodore Matthew C. Perry of the U.S. Navy visits Japan.

1930s Japan takes over parts of China.

1941 Japan attacks the U.S. naval base at Pearl Harbor, Hawaii.

1945 The United States drop two atomic bombs on Japan.

1995 An earthquake in Kobe kills more than 6,000 people.

Want to Know More?

At the Library

Bornoff, Nicholas. *Japan*. Austin, Tex: Raintree Steck-Vaughn, 1997.

Scoones, Simon. *A Family from Japan*. Austin, Tex.: Raintree Steck-Vaughn, 1998.

Streissguth, Thomas. *Japan*. Minneapolis: Carolrhoda Books, 1997.

On the Web

For more information on this topic, use FactHound.

1. Go to *www.facthound.com*
2. Type in this book ID: 0756500303.
3. Click on the *Fetch It* button.

FactHound will find the best Web sites for you.

Through the Mail
Embassy of Japan
2520 Massachusetts Avenue, N.W.
Washington, DC 20008
For information about the country

On the Road
Japan Travel Bureau
2050 West 190th Street
Torrance, CA 90504
310/618-0961
To find out about visiting Japan

Index

About the Author

Susan Sinnott has written two books in the American Girl Collection by the Pleasant Company. She has also written for Children's Press, Franklin Watts, and Millbrook Press and contributed to *Cobblestone* and *Cricket* magazines. Her *Extraordinary Hispanic Americans* was chosen as an ALA Best Reference Book of 1993. Susan Sinnott lives with her two children in Maine.